AMERICAN
DUE PROCESS

AMERICAN
DUE PROCESS

Dr. Paul A. Jones

Outskirts Press, Inc.
Denver, Colorado

American Due Process

Outskirts Press, Inc.
http://www.outskirtspress.com

ISBN: 978-1-4327-7004-4

Contents

Foreword

MY BOOK *The Myth of Rehabilitation* did not get very wide distribution. However, most of those who read it were favorably impressed. But there were some who misunderstood the emphasis. One prominent person thought that I was advocating a totalitarian system with little or no due process or human rights. This is not accurate. We need due process to prevent convicting innocent people. But there is entirely too much manipulating of the system by those who are factually guilty in order to minimize or avoid punishment. For instance, endless delays and appeals are foolish and need to be curtailed. Consequently, I am writing this sequel to clarify what changes are needed.

Many prisons and jails are too soft on the inmates. Televisions, stereos, libraries, and many other benefits abound. There are a couple of penal institutions, one in Arizona and one in North Carolina, which have dramatically reduced these benefits. However, the one in North Carolina may have gone too far. According to one television show, inmates have been physically abused, and at least one died under questionable circumstances. Of course, no reasonable person would support this type of behavior.

When an acquaintance of mine went to work for a sheriff's department in Texas, several points were made during his orientation. Two of them were: Many of the prisoners are awaiting trial, and they may or may not be guilty of anything. Others are material witnesses and may not even be involved in any wrongdoing. The implication behind these concepts was that people needed to be treated properly because they may not be guilty of anything. Actually, even guilty people should be treated properly. On the other hand, prison should be for punishment.

When I first started doing research on due process, I became more aware of the other side of the issue. While due process is often used as a gimmick by the guilty to obstruct justice—and this needs to be changed (the means whereby is the subject of this booklet)—there are still far too many places in this country where people still have their rights violated.

Introduction

Criminal justice does not mean convicting the innocent—Defense Attorney

It does not mean letting the guilty go unpunished either—Author

WHEN PEOPLE TALK about their constitutional rights, they usually mean the first ten amendments to the Constitution (The Bill of Rights), and specifically numbers IV, V, VI, VIII, and also the XIV Amendment (1868).

In my book, *The Myth of Rehabilitation (2001)*, it was suggested that the Bill of Rights should be updated to continue protecting the rights of people accused of crimes, but to minimize its use by defense attorneys and guilty people to avoid punishment, which happens all too often.

There were some objections to the idea of "tampering" with the Bill of Rights. However, the much-lauded Fourteenth Amendment was in a sense tampering, but most people consider it to be a change for the better. Many people look on the Bill of Rights as sacred, if not divinely inspired. Actually, Article V of the Constitution provides for changes (amendments), and there have been 26 changes, including the first ten.

If we want a fair and just society, we need several changes in our criminal justice system, starting with the Bill of Rights. Those guilty of wrongdoing need to be punished with as much accuracy as possible. Obviously, no reasonable person wants to punish the innocent. And we do not want to return to the vigilante system where people are punished with little or no due process or proof—just based upon an accusation.

On the other hand, tricky defense attorneys and lenient judges should not be allowed to manipulate the system (especially for the rich and famous) to allow people to escape justice. Most people accused of crimes cannot afford a defense attorney. Therefore, allowing those with money to hire one is not fair, resulting in two standards of justice—one for the poor and another for the well off. Every state should have public defenders, and everyone, rich or poor, should have to use them. There should be no defense attorneys for hire in criminal cases. Defense attorneys should be a thing of the past, except in civil cases.

Several other related changes will also be mentioned, including:
1. Punishment for lenient judges
2. Mandatory sentences
3. Appeal of acquittals
4. Required self-incrimination (Brain Mapping)
5. Sentence enhancement
6. Need for cruel and unusual punishment for cruel and unusual crimes
7. Eliminating bail and bond
8. No statute of limitations
9. No separate juvenile justice system
10. No insanity defense
11. Restorative justice

An attorney friend of mine said that our criminal justice system, while certainly not perfect, was the best in the world and also the best of all time. Unfortunately, this opinion is not that unusual. I do not know if it is the best in the world or the best there has ever been, but I doubt both assertions. However, even if both ideas are true, our criminal justice is still not very good, contrary to what they teach us in school. It is unfair, ineffective, and totally illogical. What sense does it make to execute some murderers while others are released with little or no punishment whatsoever? And why are child molesters frequently set free after short sentences when most psychologists and most molesters themselves agree that they are not "curable" and will almost always reoffend?

Our criminal justice system is very bad, and it does need improving. Some have asked whether any of the recommended changes and improvements will actually take place. Many have said that while they sound good, it is doubtful if they will happen in the near future. Perhaps they will not all happen quickly, but hopefully, most will come to pass eventually.

The Bill of Rights

THE BILL OF Rights, or the first ten amendments to the United States Constitution, is considered by many to be one of the most advanced and fairest documents in history concerning human rights. Perhaps it is, but it is not as good as it should be.

Many people believe that the Bill of Rights instantly provided due process rights to everyone in the country from the day it was ratified—to both citizens and noncitizens alike. And many textbooks seem to imply this as well. Of course, that would have been nice, but it just did not happen that way. Actually, the Bill of Rights was initially meant only to limit the power of the federal government, not that of the states. And only after its acceptance did the thirteen original colonies agree to join the Union.

In practice, most people did not benefit from the Bill of Rights for years, especially minorities. The American Indians routinely had their rights violated by both the federal and state governments until well into the twentieth century. The Chinese coolies who came to this country prior to the Civil War had almost no rights at all. And those who immigrated after that were not treated much better. Mexicans and Blacks in the South and Southwest, especially poor ones, had their rights violated as a matter of course until well into the 1960s. And these violations continue, but on a lesser scale since they are no longer officially sanctioned.

It was not until 1925 that the Supreme Court in *Gitlow v. New York* (a First Amendment case) ruled that the due process clause of the Fourteenth Amendment applied to the states as well as to the federal government. The constitutional amendments, which were originally drafted to limit the powers of the federal government, were now used by the Supreme Court to also limit the powers of the state governments as well. Of course, this was only "on paper." It was not until into the 1960s that these rights were actually enforced. This was 169 years after the Bill or Rights was ratified, 92 years after the Fourteenth Amendment, and 45 years after *Gitlow v. New York*. (Quite a long wait!)

Some of the states did give some people their due process rights prior to the 1960s. For instance, some writers believe that Lizzie Borden got away with killing her parents (1893, Mass.) because the judge did not allow the information that the investigator got from Lizzie about the crime to be used in the trial. His reason was that she had not been informed about her Fifth Amendment rights against self-incrimination prior to the interview.

We continue to hear about due process rights violations in New York, Philadelphia, New Orleans, Houston, Chicago, Los Angeles, as well as in many other places. People are denied their right to an attorney or to remain silent. They are pressured, tricked, abused, and even tortured into making confessions. Hopefully, these will grow fewer and fewer as police applicants are better screened, police activities are better monitored, and more effective punitive measures for police misconduct are put into effect.

In the 1960s, the Supreme Court got more seriously involved in state criminal law. *Mapp v. Ohio* (1961), about the exclusionary rule; *Gideon v. Wainwright* (1963), about the accused's right to counsel; and *Miranda v. Arizona* (1966), about the well-known Miranda Warning, all furthered the concept of due process in criminal law. Of course, the Fourteenth Amendment, which extended both due process and equal protection to the states, made all this possible. But it was a very long time from its inception in 1868 until the 1960s.

Summary:

1. The Bill of Rights, or the first ten amendments (passed by Congress on October 25, 1789, and ratified December 15, 1791), was originally designed to limit abuse of power by the federal government. These protections were only gradually extended to protect individuals from state governments as well.

2. Section 1 of the Fourteenth Amendment (ratified July 9, 1868) basically says that the states cannot make or legally enforce laws that take away rights given to all citizens by the federal government, and the states must also provide all citizens with due process. Of course, this was basically not enforced very well until the 1960s.

3. While we as a nation seem reluctant to admit it, there are still a lot of due process rights violations occurring. This, of course, should be dealt with. There are still many places where the need for arrest and search warrants, and the right against self-incrimination and to remain silent are routinely ignored. The guilty law enforcement personnel are often not held accountable, much less punished. And this, obviously, needs to be corrected. There needs to be a means of punishing any authorities who intentionally violate people's constitutional (due process) rights. On the other hand, there also needs to be methods of minimizing the use of due process by tricky attorneys and guilty people seeking to avoid punishment when it is proper.

The First Ten Amendments to the Constitution as Ratified by the States

These amendments were ratified December 15, 1791, and form what is known as the "Bill of Rights."

Amendment I

Congress shall make no law respecting an establishment of religion, or prohibiting the free exercise thereof; or abridging the freedom of speech, or of the press; or the right of the people peaceably to assemble, and to petition the Government for a redress of grievances.

Amendment II

A well regulated Militia, being necessary to the security of a free State, the right of the people to keep and bear Arms, shall not be infringed.

Amendment III

No Soldier shall, in time of peace be quartered in any house, without the consent of the Owner, nor in time of war, but in a manner to be prescribed by law.

Amendment IV

The right of the people to be secure in their persons, houses, papers, and effects, against unreasonable searches and seizures, shall not be violated, and no Warrants shall issue, but upon probable cause, supported by Oath or affirmation, and particularly describing the place to be searched, and the persons or things to be seized.

Amendment V

No person shall be held to answer for a capital, or otherwise infamous crime, unless on a presentment or indictment of a Grand Jury, except in cases arising in the land or naval forces, or in the Militia, when in actual service in time of War or public danger; nor shall any person be subject for the same offence to be twice put in jeopardy of life or limb; nor shall be compelled in any criminal case to be a witness against himself, nor be deprived of life, liberty, or property, without due process of law; nor shall private property be taken for public use, without just compensation.

Amendment VI

In all criminal prosecutions, the accused shall enjoy the right to a speedy and public trial, by an impartial jury of the State and district wherein the crime shall have been committed, which district shall have been previously ascertained by law, and to be informed of the nature and cause of the accusation; to be confronted with the witnesses against him; to have compulsory process for obtaining witnesses in his favor, and to have the Assistance of Counsel for his defence.

Amendment VII

In Suits at common law, where the value in controversy shall exceed twenty dollars, the right of trial by jury shall be preserved, and no fact tried by a jury, shall be otherwise re-examined in any Court of the United States, than according to the rules of the common law.

Amendment VIII

Excessive bail shall not be required, nor excessive fines imposed, nor cruel and unusual punishments inflicted.

Amendment IX

The enumeration in the Constitution, of certain rights, shall not be construed to deny or disparage others retained by the people.

Amendment X

The powers not delegated to the United States by the Constitution, nor prohibited by it to the States, are reserved to the States respectively, or to the people.

The punctuation and capitalization used here is from the original of the Joint Resolution of Congress proposing the Bill of Rights.

Non Due Process Amendments

1. Amendment I

Freedom of Religion, Speech, and the Press. Rights of Assembly and Petition

Amendment I
Congress shall make no law respecting an establishment of re-ligion, or prohibiting the free exercise thereof; or abridging the freedom of speech, or of the press; or the right of the people peaceably to assemble, and to petition the Government for a re-dress of grievances.

Even a cursory study of European history demonstrates the problems of either the church (any church) controlling the government or of the government controlling or dominating the church. We are very fortunate that our forefathers saw fit to eliminate both of these tendencies in this country. Nevertheless, there have been some unusual interpretations of this separation of church and state. One is that churches should not have to pay taxes. Another is that prayers in public schools should not be allowed.

Freedom of Religion

Many of the early settlers came to this country primarily for religious freedom. The First Amendment prohibits Congress from establishing or supporting an official church as many countries do. Freedom of religion also includes the right to worship in any manner one chooses, but some people believe that they should be allowed to do anything they wish if it is their religious belief. However, like all other rights, this one has limitations. Practices that are harmful, immoral, or otherwise illegal, such as polygamy, human sacrifice, slavery, denying needed medical care to children, or having illegal drugs or weapons are not covered by religious freedom. Freedom of religion should not mean that the government cannot regulate church schools or boarding homes. Many cases of physical, psychological, and sexual abuse have gone uncovered because the state does not monitor these institutions.

One strange interpretation of religious freedom is that of exempting churches from paying taxes. This probably needs to be looked into. Churches, church schools, and church businesses are essentially using the separation of church and state as a tax dodge. Since they benefit from police and fire protection, road and highway maintenance, and other tax-supported benefits, they ought to pay their share of taxes.

Like the other nine amendments, the First Amendment was initially designed to protect people from the federal government. Several states had laws prohibiting non-Protestants from holding public office until the mid-1800s. And both Connecticut and Massachusetts had official state churches for a long time after the Bill of Rights was ratified. Actually, it was not until in the 1920s that the Supreme Court ruled that the states also had to support the First Amendment.

A recent and unpopular interpretation of the separation of church and state is that prayers are not proper in public schools. However, there ought to be a way of resolving this intelligently, letting the majority have the type of prayers they want while exempting any who do not wish to participate or allowing them other alternatives.

Freedom of Speech and of the Press

The Founding Fathers considered both freedom of speech and of the press absolutely necessary in a democracy. Again, these freedoms are not absolute. There are laws against libel, sedition, and obscenity. Some would like to do away with these restrictions altogether. However, reasonable and limited restrictions are thought by many to be in the best interest of society in general.

2. Amendment II
Right to Bear Arms

Amendment II
A well regulated Militia, being necessary to the security of a free State, the right of the people to keep and bear Arms, shall not be infringed.

The original intent of this amendment was to prevent Congress (the federal government) from disarming state militias (the national guard). A state militia was felt necessary to keep order when needed, not as a buffer against the federal government, as some believe.

The second clause, "the right of the people to keep and bear Arms shall not be infringed," is subject to two interpretations. The first is that it is merely an explanation of the first clause, people, meaning people of the states in general, not individuals. And in the context of the times and of the other amendments, that appears to be how it was meant originally.

The second and more recent interpretation is that all citizens have a constitutional right to own, and perhaps carry, firearms. Of course, even if the first view was the original meaning, the second one might be legitimate by extension as was the case for other amendments.

Over the years, many of the limitations on the federal government have been extended to the states. The question here is whether a protection of the states from the federal government should be extended to individuals as well.

In any event, one of two things needs to be done with this amendment. Of course, no one today questions the states' right to have national guards. But it needs to be settled once and for all whether people have a constitutional right to own and carry firearms. The Supreme Court needs to say either that they do or they do not. Another option would be to clarify the second part by legislative action to specifically say individuals or to delete it entirely if that is not what is intended.

3. Amendment III
Quartering of Soldiers

Amendment III
No Soldier shall, in time of peace be quartered in any house, without the consent of the Owner, nor in time of war, but in a manner to be prescribed by law.

This amendment has no meaning or purpose in the twenty-first century. The American Army is not a foreign army of occupation. It has no policy of forcing civilians to board its troops. This amendment could be deleted altogether. Or, if it is left, it should be noted that it is only for historical interest.

4. Amendment VII
Rights in Civil Cases

> *Amendment VII*
> *In Suits at common law, where the value in controversy shall exceed twenty dollars, the right of trial by jury shall be preserved, and no fact tried by a jury, shall be otherwise re-examined in any Court of the United States, than according to the rules of the common law.*

Twenty dollars was a lot more money at that time (1798) than it is now (2011). Therefore, this amount probably should be reevaluated. This amendment provides for a jury trial in civil cases. And even though this applies only to federal courts, most state constitutions also provide for jury trials in civil cases.

5. Amendment IX
Rights Retained by the People
Powers Retained by the States

> *Amendment IX*
> *The enumeration in the Constitution, of certain rights, shall not be construed to deny or disparage others retained by the people.*

When the Bill of Rights was adopted, some people feared that listing these rights might be interpreted to mean that any not specifically listed were unprotected. This amendment was therefore adopted to prevent such an interpretation.

6. Amendment X
Powers Retained by the States and the People

The powers not delegated to the United States by the Constitution, nor prohibited by it to the States, are reserved to the States respectively, or to the people.

This amendment seems to be an extension of the Ninth Amendment. It guarantees that the federal government will not swallow up the states. However, the fact that the states retain all powers not specifically given to the federal government is complicated because the Constitution says that the federal government can make any laws that it deems "necessary and proper" to carry out its functions. This leads to differences of opinions in deciding between questions of states' rights and the ever-growing power of the federal government.

Due Process Amendments

THE FOURTH, FIFTH, Sixth, Eighth, and Fourteenth amendments are the primary ones that affect procedural due process in criminal cases. In this section, each one will be stated, briefly explained, and then commented upon, with suggestions for improvement.

1. Amendment IV
2. Amendment V
3. Amendment VI
4. Amendment VIII
5. Amendment XIV

1. Amendment IV
Search and Arrest Warrants

No unreasonable searches and seizures, and requirement of probable cause to arrest

Amendment IV
The right of the people to be secure in their persons, houses, papers, and effects, against unreasonable searches and seizures, shall not be violated, and no Warrants shall issue, but upon probable cause,

supported by Oath or affirmation, and particularly describing the place to be searched, and the persons or things to be seized.

Search Warrants

A warrant from a judge or magistrate is usually required to search someone or their property. There are some exceptions to this. Searches related to a lawful arrest, seizures of illegal property in plain view, searches when immediate action is needed, and searches that are consented to are some of them.

The Exclusionary Rule

"The exclusionary rule (1961) states that incriminating evidence found in violation of a constitutional right should not be admissible in court." "Prior to the Mapp case (1961), the exclusionary rule applied only to cases prosecuted under federal laws, based on the court's decision in *Weeks v. United States* (1914)." However, as a result of *Mapp v. Ohio* (367 U.S. 643) (1961) the exclusionary rule was extended to cases prosecuted under state laws as well.

There is still criticism of the exclusionary rule. Two of the main objections are
1. People who are actually guilty are often not prosecuted or convicted. They are turned loose to continue victimizing society.
2. The exclusionary rule has not been effective in controlling police conduct. Better ways can be utilized to teach the police a lesson other than freeing the guilty.

It seems that the best way to deal with this is to allow the evidence but also punish the offending officers with fines or suspension (and possibly prison when the offense is serious enough).

Bad Results of the Exclusionary Rule

There are numerous cases of the exclusionary rule being used for undesirable results. In 2001, a man was rearrested for the murder of two Mormon missionaries some ten years ago in Texas. He invited them over for a meal, shot them, and then dismembered their bodies. However, he was released upon appeal because it was determined that the evidence was improperly obtained—not that he was innocent.

In 1969 or 1970, John Keck was beating his wife in a drunken rage in Knoxville, Tennessee. Their daughter, a Miss Tennessee winner, called the police. However, when they arrived, they refused to enter the house without a warrant to intervene. Even though they could hear the woman's screams, they would not go in on the daughter's request, they said because she was a minor. That seemed absurd at the time—and still does. John then beat his wife to death while both the daughter and the police stood outside the door. He ended up serving five years for the murder. In this case, a woman was allowed to die because of excessive caution on the part of the police, an unfortunate misapplication of the Fourth Amendment.

Arrest Warrants

For an arrest warrant to be issued, there must be probable cause. Supposedly this would minimize arbitrary arrests used for harassment purposes—as was done in medieval Europe and still is done in many countries today. Probable cause means that the person is very likely guilty.

2. Amendment V

Rights in criminal cases

Federal Due Process, No Double Jeopardy or Self-Incrimination

Amendment V
No person shall be held to answer for a capital, or otherwise in-
famous crime, unless on a presentment or indictment of a Grand
Jury, except in cases arising in the land or naval forces, or in the
Militia, when in actual service in time of War or public danger; nor
shall any person be subject for the same offence to be twice put
in jeopardy of life or limb; nor shall be compelled in any crimi-
nal case to be a witness against himself, nor be deprived of life,
liberty, or property, without due process of law; nor shall private
property be taken for public use, without just compensation.

Federal Due Process

A Grand Jury indictment is required in federal cases. However, it is not required in state cases, and many states have discontinued its use, using a preliminary hearing instead.

Double Jeopardy

The no double jeopardy provision means that a person cannot be tried twice for the same offense by the same governmental body. He or she can be tried again if no verdict is reached, and sometimes by a different authority. Nevertheless, the double jeopardy clause needs to be eliminated, or at least modified. Of course, we do not want to try people over and over again without good reason. However, if there is new evidence indicating probable (or even possible) guilt or if the jury or judge obviously did the wrong thing, logic dictates that the suspect should be retried.

And judges can do stupid and unfair things. Take the relatively recent au pair case in Massachusetts (1997) where Judge Zobel set the killer free even though she was convicted of murder. More recently, U.S. District Judge Stewart Dalzell set Lisa Michelle Lambert free in Pennsylvania, even though she was obviously guilty as well. He took her statements as facts, even though she had demonstrated herself to be a pathological liar. A California judge only gave Tim Santee one year in jail for beating Helen Love to death in a nursing home. And there are many other similar cases, far too numerous to mention here.

Self-Incrimination

Torture or excessive pressure or trickery obviously should not be used in obtaining convictions. The reason being that there will be a lot of false convictions, and there have been in some places. However, it makes no sense for a person accused of a crime not to be required to tell the truth, whatever it is. Unfortunately, our system encourages people to lie. They are expected to deny guilt, even if they and everyone else knows that they are guilty. This is absurd, and it needs to be changed. Pleading the Fifth is a gimmick for guilty people and defense attorneys to avoid conviction and punishment. We forget that due process is supposed to ensure that the innocent are not convicted. It was never intended to help the guilty avoid punishment, as many defense attorneys believe.

Along with the above, there should be no privileged information, not for defense attorneys, spouses, doctors, priests, reporters, or anyone else. Anyone knowing about a crime should be required to tell the truth about it.

Terrorism & Torture

(Text is similar to that published in *Playboy* magazine's letters to the editor during the year of 2002 by the author.)

On Sunday, January 19, 2002, 60 Minutes *had a program about dealing with terrorists, specifically using torture in some instances to obtain critical information. This could be the identity of other terrorists or information about upcoming terrorist acts.*

A French officer on the show said that they had used torture (specifically smothering) very effectively when dealing with Algerian terrorists (prior to 1962). They obtained the identity of other terrorists and supposedly were able to prevent several terrorist acts. What was unusual was that a well-known defense attorney (noted for his stand on due process and human rights) agreed with the idea of using torture on suspected terrorists. A law school professor on the show disagreed. But it was said that Zacarias Moussaoui (the so-called 20th hijacker) should be tortured to obtain information about the identity of his collaborators and their plans.

Until recently, the CIA and our military engaged in both torture and assassinations. Often these things were done indirectly by our allies or collaborators, but not always. Supposedly, after recent legislation, we no longer engage in doing these things. However, we do accept intelligence information from places such as Jordan, Egypt, and others that do use torture to obtain it.

But now—how should we deal with known or suspected terrorists, especially in the light of September 11? Can a democratic country afford to suspend human rights or due process? And if we do, where will it end? Detaining people without charging them is a very dangerous idea, as is questioning them without letting them have an attorney. And places in Chicago, Houston, and Los Angeles have recently used torture on (nonterrorist) suspects. Perhaps they still do.

Terrorism is no good, and it needs to be stopped, but neither are police states that disregard human rights or due process as a matter of course. It doesn't matter if they are our allies or not. Communist, Islamic, or capitalistic dictatorships are still dictatorships. And we probably should oppose all of them.

3. Amendment VI
Right to a Fair Trial

Right to a Speedy Trial, Jury, and Counsel
Amendment VI
In all criminal prosecutions, the accused shall enjoy the right to a speedy and public trial, by an impartial jury of the State and district wherein the crime shall have been committed, which district shall

have been previously ascertained by law, and to be informed of the nature and cause of the accusation; to be confronted with the witnesses against him; to have compulsory process for obtaining witnesses in his favor, and to have the Assistance of Counsel for his defence.

Right to a Speedy and Public Trial

Obviously a person should be tried reasonably soon, but often they are not, for a variety of reasons.

Right to Be Tried by an Impartial Jury

This means a jury that is open-minded and not prejudiced against the defendant. However, it was not intended to mean one that is biased in favor of the defendant either. But an impartial jury is exactly what a defense attorney does not want, especially when an obviously guilty client is involved. Anytime it is obvious that a jury is biased in either direction—for acquittal or conviction—the jury should immediately be dismissed. And if the verdict is obviously in contrast to the facts, the jury should be dismissed, fined (possibly imprisoned), and the case should be retried. Meanwhile, the defendant should remain in custody. There are many cases of juries doing the wrong thing because of bias. This includes both convicting the innocent and acquitting the guilty. (Contrary to what many people think, the Sixth Amendment does not say we are to be tried "by a jury of one's peers"; only that it be impartial.)

Right to Be Tried in the State and District Where the Crime Shall Have Been Committed

However, sometimes the place where the crime was committed is so biased in favor (or against) the defendant that a fair trial is impossible. There are many examples of this. For instance, during the 1960s, some grand juries refused to indict people who murdered civil rights workers. And when indicted, many juries refused to convict. Another example is one that occurred in the 1920s near Mexia, Texas. A local man shot and killed an unarmed banker in front of several witnesses for requesting payment on a loan. He was acquitted, even though he was obviously guilty. In the 1990s, several grand juries refused to indict policemen obviously guilty of murder.

Another among thousands of cases where a jury did the wrong thing was in 1997 when Dustin Camp deliberately ran over and killed Brian Deneke in Amarillo, Texas (*Texas Monthly* 11-99). The jury did convict Dustin of manslaughter instead of murder, and then they gave him only probation (essentially nothing). This was a biased jury in favor of the perpetrator and against the victim because he was one of the outcast "punk rockers." Logically, this case should have been moved to where a fair trial could have occurred. That jury should have been dismissed. And Judge Lopez should have let the jurors' names be public instead of sealing the list for fear of retaliation for their improper decision.

Defense Attorney Warren Clark used the tried-and-proven but inappropriate trick of putting the victim on trial, causing the jury to be even more prejudiced against him. And while there were some threats of retaliation against Mr. Camp, evidently none were carried out. This case (like the Watkins case in Tarrant County) is another gross miscarriage of justice by a jury accountable to no one. The trial should never have been held there. But, after the inappropriate verdict, the killer should have been retired by an impartial court and jury, or the principle of <u>sentence enhancement</u> should have been applied. Unfortunately, the judge, the jury, and the defense attorney are accountable to no one.

Cases are sometimes moved because the accused or the defense does not feel that the defendant can get a fair trial locally. They should also be moved if prosecution cannot get a fair (unbiased) trial or if they will not do their job properly.

The accused should be informed of the charges against them, be able to confront their accuser, and have the assistance of counsel.

All of the above named provisions are important. They grew out of reaction to trials in England that could be delayed for years, and then held in secret. And the accused might never know who his accusers were, nor would he have a chance to confront them.

Many states did not provide for counsel automatically until 1963 (*Gideon v. Wainright*). However, we should do away with defense attorneys altogether because, as a rule, only the wealthy or well known have access to them. Most defendants have to use public defenders or court-appointed attorneys. This gives an unfair advantage to the rich. An intelligent and skillful defense attorney can often manipulate the court system and fool juries into acquitting or inadequately punishing those who are obviously guilty. In the interest of fairness, everyone should have to use public defenders. This would ensure an equal chance for all, rather than the wealthy often being acquitted, even when they should not be.

4. Amendment VIII

Excessive Bails, Fines, and Punishments

Bail, Fines, No Cruel and Unusual Punishment
Amendment VIII
Excessive bail shall not be required, nor excessive fines imposed, nor cruel and unusual punishments inflicted.

Excessive Bail Shall Not be Required

But exactly what is excessive bail? A wealthy person who should not be released can often secure release anyway, even with a supposedly high bail. On the other hand, a relatively poor person who might be safe to release may find it impossible to get out even with a nominal requirement. Obviously, what is excessive for one person will not be so for someone else.

Actually, the whole idea of bail (excessive or otherwise) needs to be reexamined. There probably should be no bail for murderers, child molesters, or anyone who is either violent or a flight risk. There are hundreds of examples of why this is so, but the case of Ira Einhorn who murdered his girlfriend in 1977 in Pennsylvania is one of the best. He was obviously guilty; he knew he would be convicted; and he had wealthy friends who would (and did) bankroll his flight from the country. There was no doubt that he would run away, and yet, he was released on bail anyway. And it took almost 25 years to bring him back, which is absurd. There should not be any bail for people like him. This part of the Eighth Amendment should be changed.

Like many other aspects of our criminal justice system, the application of bail is inconsistent. In practice, excessive bail is required all the time for people who obviously will not be able to make it. And for them, this has the effect of no bail at all. On the other hand, violent people and flight risks are frequently released—sometimes with disastrous results. They commit more crimes and/or disappear. And sometimes they retaliate or intimidate witnesses or accusers. The conclusion is that there should be no bail, excessive or not, for people who should not be released.

Excessive Fines Should Not Be Imposed

But who determines what is excessive? And should it be determined by the ability (inability) of the offender to pay or by the severity of the offense. This idea needs to be clarified.

Cruel And Unusual Punishment Should Not Be Inflicted (Given)

No doubt the framers of the Bill of Rights knew what they meant by cruel and unusual punishment. They probably meant torture and mutilation, as was common in Europe. However, it is not clear at the present time exactly what they meant. And attorneys and others have twisted it to mean whatever they want it to mean.

In 1972, capital punishment, as it was then imposed, was found to be cruel and unusual. However, many laws have been changed, and capital punishment is now used in several states and by the federal government. Obviously, hanging a small child for stealing a piece of bread, as was done in Medieval Europe, is excessive (cruel and unusual); so is cutting someone's hand off for stealing five dollars, as is done in some third world countries.

Concerning capital punishment, while many people are not even interested in the subject, there do seem to be three points of view among those who are. First, there are those who oppose it outright. They feel that there should be no capital punishment for anyone for anything. Then there are those who can accept the idea of capital punishment itself but are bothered by the inconsistent manner in which it is meted out. Recent findings (2001) of improper convictions of factually innocent people have added ammunition to this attitude. A third but less popular viewpoint is to favor capital punishment outright, and possibly to extend its use even further.

What is both absurd and unfair is to execute (or try to execute) some people for crimes when others who have done similar or worse offenses are not even imprisoned very long. Many killers are out in five years or less. Others are not even sent to prison. Robert Kleasen, who killed Mark Fischer and Gary Darley, two Mormon missionaries, in 1974, was released by the Court of Criminal Appeals in 1975 because of a faulty search warrant. This is a very bad way of reprimanding the police. Actually, it only punishes the public by turning loose dangerous killers among them. (There needs to be a better way of punishing the authorities for "unreasonable searches and seizures" other than not punishing guilty people.) The exclusionary rule needs to be more limited. If evidence shows a defendant to be guilty of a serious crime, it should be admissible, even if obtained under less-than-perfect circumstances.

Another example of the absurdity of our criminal justice system is the case of Paul Harington in Massachusetts. He killed his first wife and two children in cold blood thirty years ago. But he served no time because he was found not guilty by reason of insanity. Recently (2001), he killed another wife and child. This time a prosecutor was able to secure a life sentence. There should be no such thing as "not guilty by reason of insanity." If a guilty person is mentally ill, he or she should be sent to a mental hospital until stable, then he or she should serve the remainder of their sentence in prison.

Some have suggested that the cruelness and unusualness of the punishment should only be limited by the nature (cruelness and unusualness) of the crime itself. For instance, relatives and friends of victims of serious crimes such as torture and mutilation often see death by lethal injection as far too easy. Although some friends and relatives of murder and rape victims forgive the perpetrators, many feel that those who rape, torture, murder, mutilate, or cannibalize their victims should be punished as severely as possible in order to approximate what their victims suffered.

5. Amendment XIV, Section 1 (Ratified July 9, 1868)
Extending Civil Rights To All People

> *Section 1. All persons born or naturalized in the United States, and subject to the jurisdiction thereof, are citizens of the United States and of the State wherein they reside. No State shall make or enforce any law which shall abridge the privileges or immunities of citizens of the United States; nor shall any State deprive any person of life, liberty, or property, without due process of law; nor deny to any person within its jurisdiction the equal protection of the laws.*

Very few people know this, but prior to 1925, the protections of the Bill of Rights only applied to actions of the federal government. In *Gitlow v. New York* 268 U.S. 652 (1925), the court held that according to the Fourteenth Amendment, "these fundamental rights found in the first ten amendments also applied (should apply) to the states." However, very little was done to implement this decision until the 1960s. And even today, these rights are routinely denied to many.

In the 1960s, three cases stood out using the Fourteenth Amendment to extend the Bill of Rights to the states. These are:

1. *Mapp v. Ohio* 367 U.S. 643 (1961)

This case extended the exclusionary rule to the states. (See Amendment IV.)

Prior to *Mapp v. Ohio*, the exclusionary rule only applied to cases prosecuted under federal law.

2. *Gideon v. Wainwright* 372 U.S. 335 (1963)

In this case, the court held that the right to counsel was a fundamental right that should be applied to state proceedings as well as to federal cases.

3. *Miranda v. Arizona* 384 U.S. 436 (1966)

This case not only affirmed the Fifth Amendment right against self-incrimination, it also stated that a suspect must be informed of this right prior to questioning, and that he has the right to the presence of an attorney. However, overly aggressive interrogators often do not allow this.

Notes:

The Trade Center bombings, as well as the 9/11 World Trade Center and Pentagon bombings, have led to new questions about due process. Our government has come up with new ideas about dealing with terrorists at home and abroad. However, many people are concerned about the possible skimping on due process.

We do not want to convict the innocent. And there needs to be a balance between ensuring that people's due process rights are pro-tected while facilitating the conviction of guilty people.

We have made mistakes in the past, and we do not want to do anything now under the stress of the times that we will regret later. For instance, the Rosenbergs were convicted of treason and executed in 1953, even though many believe that at least the wife was not guilty. Recently, the brother, upon whose testimony they were convicted, said that he lied. Also, the internment of Japanese-American citizens during the Second World War is now considered a disgrace. And the McCarthy era is another black mark on our history. So we need to be careful how we handle suspected terrorists.

American Due Process – Part Two

V

Needed Improvements

1. Lenient Judges

2. Mandatory Sentences

3. Appeal of Acquittals

4. Double Jeopardy and Self-Incrimination

5. Sentence Enhancement

6. Cruel and Unusual Punishment

7. Bail, Bond, and Parole

8. Statute of Limitations

9. Separate Juvenile Justice System

10. Insanity Defense

11. Restorative Justice

Improvements to the Criminal Justice System

I firmly believe that there are several improvements that need to be made in our criminal justice system. However, there are those who believe that things are just fine the way they are. Some people have told me that our criminal justice system is the best in the entire world, and also the best of all times. While this is an interesting viewpoint, I totally disagree with both ideas.

I have observed how many people are offended when defendants who seem obviously guilty are acquitted. Often, these are wealthy or famous people. People's sense of fairness and justice is offended. Of course, excessively harsh punishment is also offensive, but it seems to occur less often.

All of the following suggested changes to the American criminal justice system are based on the belief that the primary purpose of the criminal justice system is to protect the public from wrongdoers and to apprehend and punish criminals. Many attorneys have told me that in their opinion this is not correct; that instead, the main function of the court system is to protect the rights of the accused. I strongly disagree and believe that that idea has led directly and indirectly to much of what is wrong with our criminal justice system, that along with the false do-gooder idea, that we should, and even can, rehabilitate criminals. Protecting the due process rights of the accused should be one function, but certainly not the primary one.

A Bill O'Reilly broadcast (December 2006) concerning cases handled by D.A. Mary Lacy of Boulder, Colorado, and Judge Edward Cashman of Vermont, leaves little doubt about our criminal justice system often being both absurd and ineffective. The following two examples should be convincing. And they are not that unusual. Numerous other examples abound.

Early in 2006, a ten-month old baby was beaten to death in Boulder, Colorado. Twenty-two bones were broken in Jason's body, including his skull. The only people in the home at the time of the murder were the parents, but the incompetent District Attorney Mary Lacy of the John Karr and Jon Benet Ramsey fame chose to ignore the case and not prosecute. It's as though the child did not matter. Ten months later, because of Bill O'Reilly's continuing to bring up the case, a grand jury was finally convened. This is the same place where a few years ago Claudine Longet, Andy Williams' former wife, shot and killed her boyfriend for threatening to leave her. She was convicted of negligent homicide (absurd) and had to serve two weeks in jail, but only at night.

Another case that Bill O'Reilly has been bothered about was the one in Vermont where two men raped and sexually abused a little girl from age seven until age ten. Judge Edward Cashman sentenced one of the perpetrators to only sixty days in jail. Why there was not a public outcry, I do not know. He was evidently one of those judges who believe in restorative justice; that pedophiles can be rehabilitated. After Bill O'Reilly complained, the sentence was increased from three to ten years. I believe the other man got thirty years. After leaving the bench, Judge Cashman taught courses in Criminal Justice at Vermont's colleges--two of which were Johnson State College and Champlain College.

1. Lenient Judges

Whenever any person or organization is not accountable to anyone, abuses can, and do, occur. This applies to medical doctors, policemen, judges, ministers, and to both religious and secular institutions. Many people will do the right thing automatically. Others may not.

Judges often seem to think that they are not accountable to anyone. Mandatory sentences would help keep criminal-coddling judges on track. But there also need to be procedures for dealing with overly lenient judges and for removing pro criminal judges.

In 2005, in the fight against organized crime, there have been cases where people who have killed several victims and committed many other felonies have been granted either immunity or minimal sentences (2002). This is wrong. How can someone who has murdered twenty or more people be set free (or placed in the witness protection program) just because he testified against (and enabled the conviction of) some organized crime leaders? No statute of limitations, no double jeopardy, along with sentence enhancement and punishment for judges and prosecutors could help rectify this.

When judges do stupid things, they are basically accountable to no one. In Alexandria, Virginia (2002), two judges returned a child to an abusive home, where she was soon murdered. But there was no penalty for the judges. And they did not even have to explain themselves. Similar cases continue to occur.

Judges need to be unglorified. They should be both accountable and more punishable when they do foolish or improper things. There need to be watchdogs for judges.

One example is the well-known 1997 au pair case in Massachusetts (Jones, p.75), where Louise Woodward was convicted of murder but was freed by Judge Hiller Zobel anyway. (In an almost identical case, the killer got twenty-five years.) Zobel has a history of overturning jury decisions, including a murder conviction. More recently, in California, a judge reduced the sentence of a couple whose dog killed a neighbor to only four years from a much longer one.

The Ohio case (11-22-00) where Judge Nadine Miller allowed the two killer-torturers of three-year-old P. J. Bourgeois to be released after less than four years is another example of a judge doing the wrong thing by allowing totally inadequate punishment to occur.

Another case of a judge doing the wrong thing is that of District Court Judge Stewart Dalzell's overturning the conviction of Lisa Michelle Lambert for murdering Laurie Snow in 1991. This decision was based on the statements of a pathological liar (the defendant herself). Fortunately, he was overturned for the time being.

Honest mistakes will happen, but there needs to be a way of

dealing with these "turn-'em-loose, Bruce" judges. This can, and should, be done although here are always those who oppose changing anything.

Probably the best way to prevent judges from giving out inappropriately lenient sentences is to have mandatory sentencing laws (see 1963).

Two things should be done. One, there needs to be procedures for removing consistently lenient judges. Two, there needs to be a method of punishing excessively lenient judges.

2. Mandatory Sentences

There is far too much discretion and variation in sentencing. Some people can get probation for murder, while others may receive relatively long sentences for theft or other nonviolent crimes. And there are still too many lenient sentences for serious crimes.

The federal courts have suggested sentencing guidelines. Unfortunately, even those are not always followed (for instance, when giving immunity or minimal sentences to dangerous people for testifying against organized crime figures).

There should be discretion for special cases, but not to the extent we now have. For instance, there are several well-known cases where children who have been severely abused have murdered their parents or guardians. And often, the children are given long prison sentences. But it does not seem right to give long prison terms to children who have been abused or tortured. There need to be provisions for dealing with these cases, especially when viewed in the light of extremely light sentences sometimes given to caretakers who kill their children. One example is the case noted in the *Chicago Tribune* of Patrick Bourgeois who was tortured to death by his parents over several months. Both were given less than four years in prison by an inefficient judicial system, including incompetent prosecutors and a judge.

The case of Helen Love, who was beaten to death by Tim Sante

(2000) in the Valley Skilled Nursing Home in Sacramento, California, illustrates the need for mandatory sentencing. He was only given one year in jail. Unfortunately, that sentence can not be lengthened, nor can that stupid judge be punished.

Another case (2004) demonstrating the unfairness, ineffectiveness, and outright stupidity of our criminal justice system is one that appeared in our local paper. A young man murdered three men in South Texas and was sentenced to life in prison. Our parole board set him free because they thought he had turned into a "good guy." He went on to graduate school and became a college processor. Mandatory sentences, no parole, sentence enhancement, and locking up permanently those who have been set free and do not deserve it would help solve the problem. (Kenneth McDuff was supposed to have become a "good guy" too.)

The State of Texas is known for giving death sentences. What is not as well known is that Texas also gives out many excessively light sentences. There are at least four well-known recent cases where people have been given probation or no time at all for murder and other serious crimes. Not only is this not fair, it just does not make sense to execute one person, give another twenty-five years, and set another free—all for doing essentially the same thing.

Mandatory Sentencing (Jewett 1983)

At first reading, O'Leary's article favoring mandatory sentencing and Kamber's article against it appear to be opposing viewpoints about what to do with the every-increasing crime problem. With a more careful reading, however, it becomes apparent that both writers favor long sentences for violent and dangerous offenders. The difference is that O'Leary believes sentences should be mandated, while Kamber wants judges and juries to have discretion.

The problem with Kamber's view is that judges and juries often give ridiculously light sentences to killers and other violent criminals—including predatory types. Some judges routinely give short sentences to young offenders, regardless of the number and severity of their crimes. They seem unaware of the fact that a fourteen-year-old can be a dangerous and hardened violent criminal who should be treated according to what he is—not what his age is. In Texas, people actually receive probation for murder. One man who beat his wife to death with a hammer was given five years' probation. Absurd!

A Mr. Reynolds, whose daughter was murdered in California, is trying to get mandatory life sentence for all third-time offenders. California and New York are pressing for this. But why wait until the third time? All predatory and violent offenders should get life sentences without the possibility of parole with their first offenses. Why should someone be allowed to kill three times or molest three children before he is put away for good? It doesn't make sense.

Mr. Kamber cites the case of Nicole Richardson—who was given a ten-year sentence for merely being an accessory to LSD distribution, as evidence against mandatory sentencing. But he is comparing unlike things (apples and oranges). First-time nonviolent offenders (including Richardson) are not what the public is worried about. They probably should not be given mandatory sentences, and probably should not serve any time at all. But killers, kidnappers, rapists, and robbers should be put away for good the <u>first</u> time. Give judges and juries the leeway, and they often will not do it. This attitude of excusing everybody for everything needs to end.

In addition to the numerous cases where guilty people are not charged, several others are given inadequate or nonexistent sentences for serious crimes. Mrs. Winkler who shot her husband in the back as he slept was only given a couple of months (Tennessee); Claudine Longet, Andy Williams' former wife, was only given a couple of weeks in jail for shooting her boyfriend and killing him after he threatened to leave her. I guess his life wasn't worth much. Perhaps mandatory sentences and sentence enhancement might help to ensure that the guilty are adequately punished.

Then, two famous examples of our weak and broken judicial system that failed to convict the obviously guilty are both the O. J.

Simpson and the Robert Blake cases. The evidence was there in both cases.

3. Appeal of Acquittals

In this country, a person can appeal his or her sentence for a crime. This would seem appropriate if the case was not handled properly or new evidence turns up. However, what usually happens is that guilty people use this to delay or inhibit justice. There are too many unnecessary and inappropriate appeals.

When an obviously guilty person is not convicted (and this happens all too often) or is sentenced too leniently, an appeal should be available to retry, re-reconvict, and resentence if necessary. Both prosecutors and victims of crimes (and their friends and relatives) should have access to this.

4. Double Jeopardy and Self-Incrimination

The provision against double jeopardy means that a person cannot be tried twice (or more often) for the same offense (7-30-06). While there may have once been legitimate reasons for not trying a person more than once, all this provision does presently is provide another means of enabling criminals and defense attorneys to escape punishment. If a jury made a stupid mistake and didn't convict when the evidence was clear or if new evidence turns up, a new trial may be in order and should be allowed.

Under the Fifth Amendment, two sections should be changed—the double jeopardy section and the self-incrimination section. Both need to be changed.

There are numerous cases when people have not been convicted but should be tried over. The fact that they have been tried once should not stand in the way if the verdict was wrong or more evidence turns up.

The public is well aware that a few years ago organized criminals made a mockery of our jury system by refusing to answer questions by claiming the Fifth Amendment entitled them to refuse to answer on the grounds that it might tend to incriminate them. Many others have used this same trick effectively. This should be changed. The original reason for having this is unclear in history; however, it serves no purpose other than giving defense attorneys and guilty people more tricks to avoid convictions.

5. Sentence Enhancement (Excessively Light Sentences)

Patricia Cornwell was on Channel 25 (5-20-08), promoting her new book. Without going into details, she made a statement that our criminal justice system is broken. Although some people are given excessively harsh sentences, far more are not caught, not charged, or not charged adequately. Many people are given minimum or no sentence at all for serious crimes.

When I was thirteen years old and living in Mexico, there was a young man who was out drinking with some buddies. For some unknown reason, he pulled out a pistol and shot to death the man across the table from him. He was never arrested and never charged with anything. He was well connected politically, and the entire thing was forgotten. I thought that this would never happen in the United States. Little did I know!

In Virginia, a former classmate of mine was divorced from his wife and a particularly nasty custody battle ensued. Evidently, he went to see his child and was looking in the window when the mother-in-law shot him between the eyes. She claimed that she thought it was a burglar, and she was acquitted.

While working for the prison system in Tennessee, I met numerous inmates who were given sentences of eleven months for manslaughter. I didn't understand it at the time, and I still don't. I had always thought that murder got you a death sentence or at least life, and that manslaughter got you seven or more years. People do get life sentences, long sentences, and death sentences, but many still get little or nothing.

When I was working in Lack Jackson in 1983, a coach at the middle school named Jackson thought that his wife was having an affair with one of her friends, and she may have been. He went to the man's house in a rage and killed him with a knife. The body was torn up so badly that the police thought he had used a shotgun. He was arrested, and he hired a school board member named Ogden Bass as his attorney. I am not sure what kind of machinations he and his friend the judge pulled off, but Jackson was soon let out of jail. The trial was delayed for over a year. Jackson was given ten years' probation with the understanding that if he didn't violate the probation it would be expunged from his record. Why did those two people think they had the right to not punish Jackson? And why did the state law allow it? Furthermore, why didn't anyone object?

A short time after the above-mentioned incident, a man beat his wife to death with a baseball bat, for which he was given five years' probation.

Another case occurred in Dallas that is interesting but not unusual. A man shot his wife in front of the children and then left, came back with a reloaded weapon, and killed her. He too was given probation. The latest case of interest is the one where a wife was convicted of murdering her husband, but the jury gave her probation.

An Eye for an Eye—At Least

The Old Testament talks about an eye for an eye as a general rule for punishment. However, many do not understand that this is a limiting recommendation, rather than a requirement for the severity of punishment. For example, if someone put your eye out, the punishment should be to put his eye out—but no more. His entire family should not be killed as had previously been the practice.

Probation for Murder. What kind of stupid system do we have

when someone can get probation for murder? Or six months? Or six years? Or whatever? Logically, the only reasonable and fair punishment for murder is capital punishment. And if we aren't going to do that we should have a life sentence with no parole or benefits—much like they have in Japan. There should be no visits, no movies, no recreation, no letters, and no music. They should be locked up in a small cell to suffer for what they have done.

The principle of sentence enhancement means that there should be a list of appropriate sentences for all crimes (mandatory sentences). When a person is convicted of a crime and the sentence falls short either due to the judge or the jury, a higher authority (of sentencing equity) would intervene and impose the appropriate sentence. This should stop someone from doing only two months for shooting her husband in the back, prevent an au pair from only serving one year for killing a baby, and other grossly inadequate sentences for serious crimes, especially homicides. The sentence enhancement board could review any inadequate sentence and impose the correct and reasonable sentence. Law enforcement, victim's relatives, or even concerned citizens could apply to the board.

6. Cruel and Unusual Punishment

Cruel and unusual punishment is prohibited by the Eighth Amendment. But it is neither explained nor is any example given; therefore, it is left up to the interpretation or imagination of whomever is deciding what it means. And, many of the interpretations are abused.

The Kenneth Allen McDuff case is an outstanding example of exactly how inadequate and dysfunctional the criminal justice system is in dealing with criminals in general and serial killers in particular. After a long history of burglary, rape, torture, and several brutal murders, he was released over and over, even though he was sentenced to death more than once.

Finally, he was given the death penalty and was executed in 1998 by lethal injection. Several family members of his victims were there. So were some of his own family. One relative of a victim who had been kidnapped, brutalized, raped, and tortured for over a week before he killed her commented that McDuff's quick-and-easy death did not seem appropriate or adequate for what he had done. There was no pain and little discomfort compared with what his victims had gone through. It was similar to being put to sleep for an operation, only he didn't wake up.

While either drawing-and-quartering or burning people at the stake may be cruel and unusual punishment, it seems that it would be a good idea for the punishment to fit the crime more closely. People who abuse and torture should probably be abused and tortured. You wouldn't want to hang a hungry child who stole a loaf of bread as was done in the Middle Ages, but a simple lethal injection is not adequate or fair to a homicide victim who was tortured to death.

7. Bail, Bond, and Parole

Perhaps bail or bond would make sense for someone who had committed a minor offense. However, it makes no sense whatsoever for repeat offenders, violent offenders, or escape risks. And there are numerous cases on record of people in these categories who just took off, even leaving the country and never returning. They should have stayed locked up.

Parole is one of the stupidest ideas we have in the criminal justice system. The Kenneth Allen McDuff case is one of the best examples of this. He was let out time and again to kill over and over—although he had been given both life and death sentences. And there are numerous other similar examples. Turning dangerous people loose to prey on society is the best reason for not having any parole.

The second reason for not having parole is that it enables people to avoid serving the sentence they deserve, regardless of whether they are dangerous. Some forty years ago, a boy (named Cross) killed two girls, stuffed them into his closet, and then went out on a date. Although he should have been executed, he received a life sentence. But the parole board let him out after thirty years, and he went to live with his family in Dallas. Is he still dangerous? Probably. But we may never know.

Examples abound, but both parole and parole boards should be abolished.

8. Statute of Limitations

What the statue of limitations means is that after the passing of a certain amount of time—three years, seven years, or whatever—a person can no longer be charged or convicted of a crime. The rational behind why we have this is somewhat unclear. It serves no useful purpose. What it does do is to allow criminals, child abusers, and others to escape punishment if enough time passes. This is unreasonable, unfair, and should be done away with.

9. Separate Juvenile Justice System

I remember reading about hungry young children being executed in Medieval times for stealing a piece of bread. We don't know for sure how accurate those accounts were nor how often it happened, but this punishment seems extremely excessive compared to modern thinking. On the other hand, the do-gooder mentality of some reformers has led to the idea that people under a certain age (18, 16, 8, 6, or whatever) are less responsible for their actions than adults because they don't fully understand what they are doing. Therefore, they should have a different court system and a different penal system.

Actually, they do understand; they do know what they're doing; and they should be held to the same standard of accountability as adults. Children, senile elderly people, the mentally retarded, and the insane should all be punished for what they do, not for whether someone believes they fully understand what they are doing—as is the current thinking.

We should do away with the juvenile justice system altogether. Giving juvenile offenders more lenient sentences than adults is foolish, unfair, and serves no useful purpose. Keeping their records sealed is also useless. All it does is keep needed information from law enforcement and the courts—causing many problems too numerous to mention here.

Having different jails and prisons for juveniles is probably all right for logistical reasons just as having different places for males and females is useful. One exception might be proper. A different court and prison system for statutory offenders would be appropriate. Runaways, truants, and any other offenders would not even be considered criminals if they were adults and should not be dealt in the same way as killers, rapists, robbers, etc.

10. Insanity Defense

Many legal books state that the insanity defense is seldom used, and when it is used it is seldom effective. However, I can recall many cases where it was used both effectively and inappropriately. The truth of the matter is that there are many people in prison who are obviously insane. At the same time, there are many who escaped punishment by claiming mental illness, and it is obvious that they are not insane.

What we should do is not have an insanity defense that enables people to escape punishment. They should be punished based upon what they did. If they are truly mentally ill, they should be sent to a mental hospital. If and when they are cured (deemed no longer insane), they should go to prison to complete their sentence.

11. Restorative Justice (Stupidity—Not Justice)

This idea of restorative justice has likely been around in one form or another for years. However, it was probably in the 1960s that people in positions of authority bought into the concept on a large scale. Many doctors, lawyers, judges, social workers, college professors, religious leaders, and others have accepted the concept to a greater or lesser extent.

What is this restorative justice? It is the opposite idea from the traditional thinking, that people who do wrong should be punished. These misguided do-gooders want to help the perpetrators instead of punishing them. They want to understand why they did what they did and how we can help them to become good or at least better people.

Examples of this thinking are: the Boston nanny who was freed even though she was convicted of murdering a baby, the man in California who received only a one-year sentence for beating a nursing home patient to death, recent cases in Vermont and Ohio where child rapists and abusers receive probation, a $25 fine, or only 30 days for their crimes. These are all examples of a system that wants to "help" the offenders but cares little or nothing about victims.

Some sort of mandatory sentencing laws would help, but there needs to be an effective way of removing ineffective judges and prosecutors.